QUESTIONS for REBEL GIRLS

Good Night Stories for Rebel Girls and all other Rebel Girls titles are available for bulk purchase for sale promotions, premiums, fundraising, and educational needs.
For details, write to sales@rebelgirls.com.

www.rebelgirls.com

Art director: Giulia Flamini
Cover: Annalisa Ventura
Graphics designers: Annalisa Ventura, Hannah Naughton
Contributors: Abby Sher, Maithy Vu, Sarah Parvis
Special thanks: Grace House, Jody Corbett, Marina Asenjo

Printed in China
First edition, 2021
10 9 8 7 6 5 4 3 2 1

ISBN: 978-1-953424-10-5

Dear Rebel Girls,

Can you picture yourself as a pirate, pop star, or pole-vaulter? Do you want to explore your personality and your hopes for the future? Who doesn't?!

WHO is your all-time hero?
WHAT makes you laugh?
WHERE would you rather go: the movies or the moon?

Here at Rebel Girls, we love asking questions. They can help you understand your fears, your curiosities, and all the things that make you so uniquely you!

We also love celebrating the strength, skills, and determination of extraordinary Rebel Women from the past and present. That's why many of the questions in this book are inspired by them. What would you do if you were in their place? Ask your friends! Ask your neighbors! Ask your great-aunt Fran with the lopsided glasses! Most of all, ask yourself.

And don't worry if you can't come up with answers right away. That's the most delicious part of asking questions! You get to explore your imagination and learn about yourself and the world around you. Just keep asking, answering, and having fun.

Enjoy!

Singer and activist LADY GAGA has said, "Kindness heals the world. Kindness heals people. It's what brings us together—it's what keeps us healthy."

What is something kind you have done for another person recently? How did it make you feel?

What do you do when someone is unkind to you?

If you had an unlimited budget to do something kind for every single person in your school, what would you do?

ADA LOVELACE

loved trying to figure out how machines work.
She wrote the first computer program ever!

If you were going to invent a machine,
what would you want it to do?

How many machines do you think you use
in an average day? Which is your favorite?

Some scientists predict that computers will one
day be smarter than humans. Do you agree or
disagree? Is that exciting or scary?

Would you rather hear a roomful of people laughing or a single voice calling your name?

Would you rather run a mile every day or stand on one foot for an hour each day?

Would you rather be a reporter sharing facts or a storyteller making up an imaginary world?

What character from a book would you want to be friends with and why?

—Penny, 8, Fort Collins, Colorado, USA

MAE JEMISON

was the first Black woman
to go to space. One of the things
she studied aboard the space shuttle was
weightlessness and its effects on astronauts.

Some astronauts have worked on growing plants
aboard spacecraft. Others have studied deserts, glaciers,
coral reefs, and other features of Earth from space.

- If you went to space, what would you like to study?

- What do you think would be the hardest part about living on a space shuttle?

- Would you rather live on a space station for a month or live on a submarine for a month?

If you were in the space shuttle about to set off for space like Sally Ride, what would you do or think about to help calm your nerves?

—Marlo, 10, Tulsa, Oklahoma, USA

KAYLA HARRISON is a sixth-degree black belt in judo. She won gold medals in the 2012 and 2016 Olympic Games. Before winning her first Olympic medal, she made sure to wear her lucky socks, which were given to her by her grandmother years before.

★ Do you have a lucky object? Why do you think it is lucky?

★ Do you do anything special before a big test, game, or performance to help you do well?

★ Do you believe that objects or rituals can bring you luck?

Rock star **JOAN JETT** says that her guitar is like a part of her body.

★ What do you think she means by that?

★ Is there anything—like a pen, lacrosse stick, telescope, or other object—that feels like a part of who you are?

IF YOU COULD MEET ANY WOMAN FROM ANY COUNTRY AND ANY TIME IN HISTORY, WHO WOULD IT BE? WHAT WOULD YOU ASK HER?

SHAILENE WOODLEY is a talented actress and a passionate advocate for the environment. She's also deeply afraid of flying. Fear of flying is a common phobia. (A *phobia* is an extreme, often irrational, fear of something—like spiders, heights, or peanut butter sticking to the roof of your mouth).

⭐ Do you have any phobias?

⭐ Does anyone in your family?

⭐ Shailene once said she might learn how to pilot a plane to help her get over her fear. What would you do to try to get over your fears?

ANITA SARKEESIAN was upset when she noticed that there were hardly any female characters—especially strong ones—in video games. So she started a blog to talk about how women are portrayed in pop culture.

⭐ What's something you've noticed that's bothered you?

⭐ If you designed a video game, what would the characters be like?

⭐ If you created a blog, what would it be about?

Actress **LUPITA NYONG'O** said, "No matter where you're from, your dreams are valid."

YEAH

Where did you grow up?
What is your **favorite memory**
of living there?

What are some of
your dreams for
the future?

Who do you share
your dreams with
and why?

You are about to go onstage.
Would you rather no one showed up or
everyone you've ever known showed up?

★

Would you rather you forgot your
lines or forgot your costume?

★

If you knew you would not win
a talent competition,
would you compete anyway?

★

If you were a judge at a talent show and
someone you didn't like did the best job,
but a good friend gave an okay performance,
who would you choose as the winner?

If your favorite sport was turned into a movie, would
you audition for it? What role would you go after?
Why would you choose that role?

—*Cadence, 10, San Luis Obispo, California, USA*

Jane Goodall devoted her life to studying chimpanzees.

IF YOU DEDICATED YOUR LIFE TO ONE TYPE OF ANIMAL, WHAT WOULD IT BE?

PAULA NEWBY-FRASER

is a triathlete, which means she competes in races
that include swimming, cycling, and running!

Would you rather compete in a triathlon
or just one event?

If you had to compete in a swimming, cycling,
or running race, which would you pick?

If you could create a race made up of any
three activities, what would they be?

Do you think it is better to be good
at many things or an expert in one thing?

Before **FUNMILAYO RANSOME-KUTI** was a powerful activist, she was a little girl in Nigeria. At the time, there were no schools for girls near her home. So her parents sent her to an all-boys school.

⭐ How would you feel about attending an all-boys school?

⭐ What about an all-girls school?

⭐ If you could create your own school, how would it be different from the school you go to now?

When **MATILDE MONTOYA** was barred from finishing medical school in Mexico because she was a girl, she wrote to the president of the entire country, asking him to step in on her behalf. And he did!

★ Who can you ask for help when you feel like you're being treated unfairly?

★ If you could ask the leader of your country any question right now, what would it be?

18

JULIA CHILD was not only a terrific chef, she was also a spy during World War II! **What are two professions you'd love to try that don't necessarily go together?**

JILL TARTER is an astronomer who searches for signs of life in outer space. She is sure there are living things on a planet somewhere.

- What do you think about there being life on other planets or out in space?

- If you met an alien, what do you think you'd do or say?

- If you were an alien, what would you think about Earth?

- If scientists discovered life on another planet, how would you react? What if they found microscopic bacteria and not walking, talking "aliens?"

What STEM subjects and techniques would you rather pursue?

ROSELI OCAMPO-FRIEDMANN

was a botanist. She was an expert in algae and microorganisms found in harsh environments.

SARA SEAGER

is an astrophysicist. She searches for life on planets outside of our solar system.

PATRICIA BATH

was an ophthalmologist. She studied and treated eye diseases and invented a device to help restore people's sight.

DR BATH

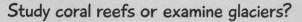

Study coral reefs or examine glaciers?

Go on an archaeological dig in the desert or work in an arctic research lab?

Gather soil samples or collect insect specimens?

Study rocks or study leaves?

Scrutinize cells or monitor lightning?

Inspect a volcano or explore a cave system?

Diagnose diseases or search for new planets?

Research reptiles or inspect algae?

Develop new fabrics or create new computer languages?

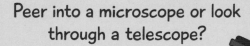

Peer into a microscope or look through a telescope?

21

AMELIA EARHART said, " Adventure is worthwhile in itself. "

Do you agree with Amelia? Do you like the time spent on the way to a destination? Or would you rather get to your destination and then start having fun?

Have you ever been on an adventure that changed the way you saw the world? What happened?

What is one thing you would take with you no matter where you were traveling?

RAPELANG RABANA is an

entrepreneur. She co-founded an internet phone service company and an online learning company.

⭐ Can you imagine running your own business?

⭐ What kind of business would you like to start?

AGATHA CHRISTIE was

a famous mystery writer. She created many characters, including two beloved detectives: Hercule Poirot, a dramatic Belgian sleuth with a pointy mustache, and Miss Marple, a woman from a small English village who likes to knit, garden, gossip, and solve crimes.

⭐ What kind of detective character would you invent?

⭐ Who in your family would make the best detective?

⭐ Who in your family could come up with the best detective stories?

CAROLINA GUERRERO

started a storytelling podcast called *Radio Ambulante* so people who speak Spanish could share their stories.

What is your native language?

⭐

How do you feel when people around you are speaking a different language than you?

⭐

How do you communicate besides using words?

⭐

If you could learn any other language, what would it be? Why?

Would you rather dream every single night knowing that you'll have nightmares sometimes, or never dream at all and never have any nightmares?

Do you have any food allergies? Do any of your friends or family? What would you be willing to give up so that you or someone you love would no longer have allergies? Would you give up your favorite food? Would you agree to never listen to your favorite band again?

Would you rather have to eat breakfast foods for at least two meals a day or never get to eat breakfast foods at all?

In most places in the United States, teenagers cannot drive until they are 16 years old. If you could make the driving age younger, would you?

Would you rather never be able to eat potato chips again or never be able to eat chocolate again?

—*Lucy, 10, Mansfield, Connecticut, USA*

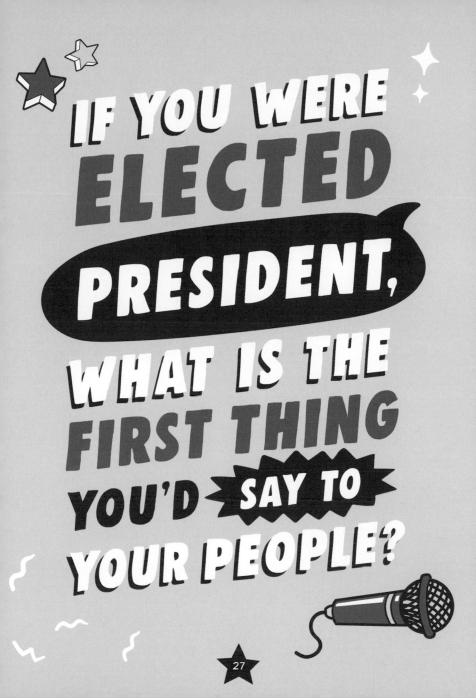

IF YOU WERE ELECTED PRESIDENT, WHAT IS THE FIRST THING YOU'D SAY TO YOUR PEOPLE?

TEMPLE GRANDIN is a scientist who advocates for the humane treatment of animals. She also speaks openly about having autism. She invented a hug machine to help her relax.

⭐ If you could create any kind of device that would help people relax, what would it be, and how would it work? What would you call your calming machine?

⭐ If you could ask Temple any question about autism, what would it be?

SOJOURNER TRUTH

traveled across the country, telling people what it was really like to be enslaved and fighting for equality. If you could travel all over telling people the truth about something, **what would it be, and what would you say?**

MARY EDWARDS WALKER was a brilliant doctor who saved many lives during the US Civil War, but she didn't dress like other women at the time. Instead of petticoats and tight corsets, she wore shirts, pants, and boots. But she ended up getting arrested for wearing men's clothes!

★ Have you ever felt like your clothes made it hard to do what you wanted to do?

★ What do you think your clothes say about who you are?

★ How would you react if your school announced that it was going to require all students to wear uniforms?

★ If you could design a school uniform for everyone in your school, what would it look like?

Would you be able to live without candy?
—*Olivia, 9, Willemstad, Curaçao*

INSPIRED

THE FOUNDERS OF REBEL GIRLS

crowdfunded their best-selling book *Good Night Stories for Rebel Girls*. That means they asked the public to donate money so they could create their book—100 tales of extraordinary women, all written in a fairy-tale style. People loved the idea and donated a TON of money for the project.

If you could crowdfund any project, what would it be?

How would you explain your idea so people would want to support it?

Andrée Peel risked her life fighting for her country's freedom. Would you choose the fate of your country over your own fate?

—Bex, 11, Laurel, Maryland, USA

EDMONIA LEWIS was a sculptor of West Indian and Chippewa heritage. Her birth name was Wildfire, but she took on the name Edmonia Lewis while in college.

Have you ever wanted to change your name? What made you feel that way? What name did you want to have instead?

What is something you like about your name?

ALFONSINA STRADA was a cyclist who was so fast and fearless that newspaper writers nicknamed her "the devil in a dress." **What would your cycling nickname be?**

Environmental pioneer **RACHEL CARSON** once said, "In nature, nothing exists alone."

What do you **think** Rachel meant?

What role should humans play in taking care of the environment?

How does nature take care of you?

What is one thing you can do right here, right now, to help the Earth?

Which is worse—oversleeping or waking up way too early?

★

Would you rather have feet like a bear or hands like a sloth?

★

Would you rather have a teacher who yelled all the time or a teacher who always whispered?

Would you rather eat earthworms or have extra homework?

—Clara, 15, Jackson, Wyoming, USA

CLEMANTINE WAMARIYA

is an author and activist who believes that stories can
connect us all and help us find courage and hope.

Do you think stories connect people? How so?

Which do you like more—listening to real-life
stories or made-up ones?

What kind of stories make you
feel more hopeful?

Do you like stories that end happily
ever after? Why or why not?

LAKSHMI BAI was a 19th century Indian queen and a warrior. She was so fierce that one of the generals who opposed her called her "the most dangerous of all the rebel leaders."

★ If someone described you, what are three adjectives they might use?

★ Would your classmates or teammates use the same words to describe you that your family would use?

★ Imagine you ran a kingdom 200 to 300 years ago. Would you rather stay in your palace and rule or ride into battle to protect your people?

★ If you had to go to battle, would you rather be a sword fighter or an archer?

In 2020, playwright **LARISSA FASTHORSE** won a Genius Grant. That's an award given to 20 to 30 people in the United States each year to honor their "extraordinary originality and dedication in their creative pursuits." It comes with $625,000 paid out over five years.

★ If you won a lot of money for something you are good at, would you use the money to keep pursuing that talent? If not, what would you use it for?

★ The committee that picks the winners of the Genius Grant looks for people who are good at "self-direction." Are you good at motivating yourself? Or do you need a parent, teacher, or other person to give you deadlines and push you to finish things?

ROSA PARKS

kicked off an important boycott when she refused to move to the back of a bus. What's something you see as unfair that you'd like to say **NO** to right now?

MARIA MONTESSORI was an educator who believed that kids learn best by doing things themselves.

WHAT IS SOMETHING YOU TAUGHT YOURSELF TO DO?

If you could live anywhere in the world, where would it be and why?

—*Maila, 10, Honolulu, Hawaii, USA*

New Zealand's prime minister **JACINDA ARDERN** put her country on lockdown when the coronavirus pandemic hit. Everyone had to stay inside unless their job was essential or they needed to shop for necessary supplies.

- Would you have done the same thing as a leader? Why or why not?

- What were the worst parts of the pandemic for you? Were there any upsides to spending so much time at home?

- Jacinda Ardern's motto is "Be strong, be kind." How do you think people can put more kindness into the world? What's a motto that you live by?

There are so many jobs and hobbies in the world! Which would you pick?

MAUD STEVENS WAGNER

was a tattoo artist.

SARA MAZROUEI

is a planetary geologist.

JOHANNA NORDBLAD

is an ice diver.

Minecraft master or pizza chef?

Champion pole-vaulter or presidential speechwriter?

International spy or children's toy maker?

Librarian or dentist?

Professional bird-watcher or celebrity eyebrow stylist?

Video game sound designer or mountaineer?

Garden designer or prom dress designer?

Welder or bus driver?

Scuba instructor or helicopter pilot?

Pet groomer or chess player?

Which is your top pick? Why?

CARMEN HERRERA is an artist who uses lines and shapes to create abstract art. She has said, "I believe that I will always be in awe of the straight line. Its beauty is what keeps me painting."

Do you prefer abstract art or paintings that are realistic? Why?

What is the most interesting piece of art you've ever seen?

If you were to create a piece of abstract art, how would you decide what to make?

YEAH

Do you think paintings need to be beautiful?

If you were a visual artist, what materials would you use? Charcoal? Paints? Clay? Found objects? Something else?

WHAT DOES YOUR HERITAGE MEAN TO YOU?

HOW DOES IT AFFECT YOUR DAY-TO-DAY LIFE?

JANE AUSTEN was a British author who came up with timeless stories by observing the world around her. She made every detail—like the sound of a sigh or the look of a fireplace—important.

- If you wrote a story about your life, what details about your bedroom would you include to tell the reader something about you?

- What details about your school would you include?

- In describing yourself, what details about your face would you include?

I learned about Italian fencer Bebe Vio, who lost her arms and legs when she was little because she got sick. She didn't let that stop her from being a champion. What challenge have you overcome that made you feel like a winner?

—*Oakley, 8, Plantation, Florida, USA*

Would you rather be able to stay up all night and still feel okay in the morning or be able to fall asleep the minute you climb into bed and feel amazing the next day?

★

Would you rather speak only in rhymes or hiccup every time you said the word "the"?

★

Would you rather be able to change your height every day or change your hair color and style every day?

★

Would you rather be able to understand what people were saying no matter the language they were speaking or be able to understand what animals were thinking?

If you could meet only one Rebel Girl, who would you choose?

—Molly, 8, Haddon Township, New Jersey, USA

MICHELLE OBAMA'S

mother would often say to her, "If it can be done, you can do it."
She listened to her mother and grew up to be a talented lawyer
and an influential First Lady of the United States.

FADUMO DAYIB

was Somalia's first female presidential candidate.
Her mother always said to her, "You hold all life's
possibilities in the palm of your hands."

What is something your mother or other beloved
grown-up says that inspires you?

What advice will you give to your own child,
if you have one, in the future?

MARJANE SATRAPI is an Iranian artist and writer who lived through a revolution. She wrote and illustrated a graphic novel, *Persepolis*, about the dangers she witnessed as a child in Iran.

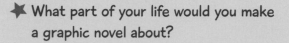

★ What part of your life would you make a graphic novel about?

★ Marjane has said that as a child she had no toys but lots of books. If you could grow up with only toys or only books, what would you pick?

★ She has also said that when she was young, she discovered how to cheat at cards. She'd cheat all the time so she could win. Do you ever cheat at games? If you could cheat and not get caught, would you?

★ After Marjane moved from Iran to Austria, she had culture shock. That means she felt disoriented being in a place completely different from what she was used to. Have you ever experienced culture shock?

When singer **ARETHA FRANKLIN** was a kid, her father hired a piano teacher to work with her. But Aretha hid when the teacher showed up! She preferred to "play by ear."

⭐ Are you like Aretha? Do you prefer to learn things on your own or attend classes and learn from experts?

MARY ANNING

was a paleontologist and fossil collector who uncovered the bones of dinosaurs. **What would you do if you found dinosaur bones?**

HEDY LAMARR was a brilliant inventor who also happened to be a beautiful actress. Lots of people—including her husband!—thought she was just pretty and couldn't possibly have great ideas too.

Have you ever been judged by your looks? Have you judged someone else by theirs? What happened?

How do you think people are treated differently based on their appearance? Do you want to change that? How can you change it?

MERRITT MOORE

is an quantum physicist *and* a professional ballerina! When she was little, people used to tell her she had to choose between pursuing physics or ballet, but she was too passionate about both to give up either. **Have you ever had to make tough choices about hobbies that you enjoy? How did you make your decision?**

BEVERLY LORAINE GREENE

was an architect. Historians think that, in 1942, she was the first Black woman to become a registered architect. She designed an arts complex, a theater, the headquarters for a major international organization, and even a funeral home.

★ If you could design any kind of building, what would you choose? What features would you include to make your building unique?

★ If you could design a house for yourself, what would it look like?

★ Would you rather design a treehouse or a castle?

★ Architects used to draw everything by hand. Now they mostly use computers. Which skill would you rather learn?

MADONNA said,
"I've been popular and unpopular, successful and unsuccessful, loved and loathed, and I know how meaningless it all is."

When was a time you felt **successful**? How did it affect your behavior?

What does "being popular" mean to you? Is being popular important? Who do you think is the most popular person in your life?

Can you describe what it feels like to be truly **loved**? Who is someone you find easy to love?

What is most important—to be popular, successful, or loved?

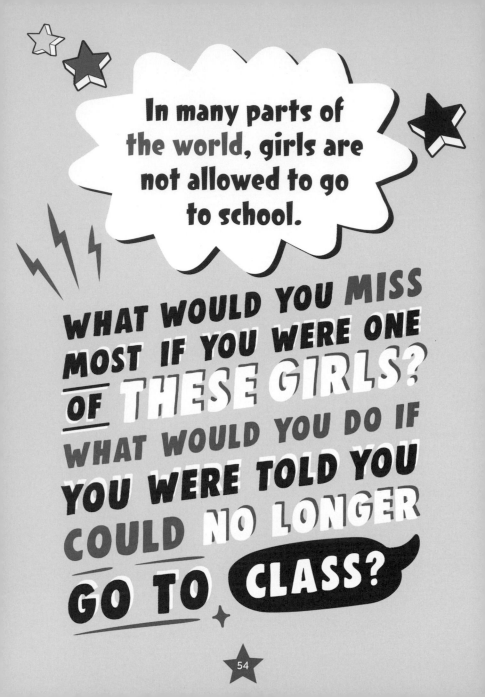

In many parts of the world, girls are not allowed to go to school.

WHAT WOULD YOU MISS MOST IF YOU WERE ONE OF THESE GIRLS? WHAT WOULD YOU DO IF YOU WERE TOLD YOU COULD NO LONGER GO TO CLASS?

If you were an astronaut, which planet would you want to fly to first?

—*Charlotte, 6, Eastampton, New Jersey, USA*

In 2018, **JEANETTE EPPS** was going to become the first Black crew member on the International Space Station. She was very excited! She'd spent years training for a mission like this! But at the last minute, NASA changed the plan and sent a different astronaut instead. She had to deal with being disappointed and trying to be patient while waiting for her next chance to go into space.

* When was the last time you were really disappointed about something? How did you deal with it?

* Do you have any pointers for other people dealing with bad news?

* Would you describe yourself as a patient person?

Who has been a very important person
in your life and why?
—*Caitlin, 7, Melbourne, Australia*

Chef **DANIELA SOTO-INNES** always makes sure that the kitchens she manages are full of laughter, dancing, and singing.

⭐ If you were the owner of a business, how would you want your employees to feel?

⭐ Do you ever dance or sing while you are doing something else?

⭐ Would you rather be the boss of a company and have to deal with the stress or be a worker at a company who can just go home at the end of the day and not think about the business?

When she was a little girl, **HILLARY CLINTON** was bullied by some children in her neighborhood. One day, her mother saw her running from her bullies. Instead of letting her hide from them, her mother sent her back outside to confront them. "You have to face things and show them you're not afraid," she told Hillary.

★ Do you think her mother gave Hillary good advice?

★ What would you do if you were in that situation?

★ Have you ever been bullied?

★ What would you do if you saw someone being bullied at school?

CLARA JULIANA GUERRERO LONDOÑO

moved to a brand-new country hoping to become a bowling champion . . . and it worked!

★ What's a dream that you would move to a new country for?

★ What do you think would be the hardest part about living in a foreign country?

★ Would you rather spend a week at bowling camp or at horseback-riding camp?

Would you rather try liver-flavored chewing gum or pickle-flavored chewing gum? Black bean-flavored gum or minty-banana?

Would you rather have a skateboard stunt or a newly discovered planet named after you?

Would you rather be able to do 100 pull-ups in a row or win 100 levels on your favorite video game?

If you could write an issue of any comic, what comic would you pick?

GRL PWR

You are a stowaway on a pirate ship and get caught. Would you rather walk the plank or get left stranded on a deserted island?

—*Molly, 11, Bismarck, North Dakota, USA*

LADI KWALI was a Nigerian artisan. She mastered all sorts of ways to make pots for cooking and pottery for decorating people's homes. She used her hands to mold and coil clay into teapots, plates, jugs, and more. She knew old-fashioned and modern techniques and mixed and matched them to come up with her own style. Ladi decorated her pottery with animals, like lizards, scorpions, and birds. She also used sleek geometric patterns.

- What do you like to make with your hands?

- Imagine you are competing to design the coolest teapot. What images or patterns would you add to your entry?

- Nigeria honored Ladi Kwali by putting her image on their currency, the naira. She is the only woman on a naira note. Do you think that is a big honor?

- Who else would you like to put on a coin or dollar bill?

MARIA CALLAS was an opera singer who moved people with her sensational voice.

OLGA KORBUT dazzled audiences as a gymnast when she spun and flipped around the uneven bars.

When all eyes are on you, what's your performing style?

Sing opera or do modern dance?

Do a magic show or put on a rap concert?

Perform a tap dance routine or
act in a one-person show?

Design the costumes or build the sets?

Direct a play or direct a movie?

Play the tuba or play the flute?

Dance in a water ballet or leap off the high dive?

Do a routine on the balance beam
or compete on the uneven bars?

Host a talk show or be a guest?

Play the harp or play the bagpipes?

Sing in a musical or be in a clown show?

Tennis player NAOMI OSAKA has said, "I play better when I'm calm. There is an inner peace I can tap into sometimes during my matches."

What can you picture in your head that calms you when you are feeling nervous?

Is there any activity that you do (or can imagine doing) that would give you a feeling of inner peace?

Which is worse: feeling nervous or having the flu?

Is it more fun to play sports with an audience watching or not?

GLADYS KALEMA-ZIKUSOKA

is a wildlife veterinarian in Uganda, where she treats endangered mountain gorillas. When Gladys was a child, she'd stay home when her pets were sick.

⭐ Do you have pets? What do you do to keep them safe and happy?

⭐ If you could have any type of pet, what would it be? What would you name it?

SHAMSIA HASSANI paints

murals in Afghanistan and around the world that show how strong women are changing the world.

⭐ What are some of your favorite pictures of strong women?

⭐ If you were going to paint a mural, what would it be of and why?

In the late 1760s, **JEANNE BARET** was the first woman to sail around the world—but she had to disguise herself as a man in order to do it! Throughout history there have been many things that women weren't allowed to do, like vote, go to school, or even wear pants!

 Imagine you lived at the same time as Jeanne. Would you do what she did? Why or why not?

 What would you do if someone announced that girls were no longer allowed to wear shorts or pants (including jeans!) in public?

 What would be the best part of sailing around the world? What would be the worst?

 What are some things you enjoy doing that used to be outlawed for women?

Is it okay to hit someone back if they hit you first?
—*Ripley, 5, Manila, Philippines*

Would you rather wear fancy clothes every day or never, ever be able to wear fancy clothes?

Would you rather have to wear a sweat suit to school every day or dress up in costumes every day?

Would you rather have Halloween once a month or Thanksgiving once a month?

What items do you think your family would bury you with, if you were in Egyptian times?

—Olivia, 13, Surrey, UK

Singer **GLORIA ESTEFAN** was very shy until she found her love of music. Music gave her an outlet to express her feelings and emotions.

- What song makes you feel fabulous inside?

- What song makes you cry?

- Is there a song you know all the lyrics to? What is it?

- If you made an album, what would you call it?

As a student, **YOKY MATSUOKA** built a robotic arm to help people who have had strokes learn to use their muscles again.

- If you built a robotic device, what would you use it for?

- What's something you would like to do to help others?

67

ANNE HIDALGO,
the mayor of Paris,
had a vision for

" a green city where
we can all breathe fresh air,
share open space, and enjoy
our lives. "

Can you think of something that would help make your city or town more green?

If you designed a public park, what would you add to make sure people would come and enjoy it?

Paris is known for the Eiffel Tower, the Louvre museum, tasty baguettes, buttery croissants, and cutting-edge fashion. What is your city or town known for?

What is missing in your hometown? If you could blink and make something appear nearby, what would it be?

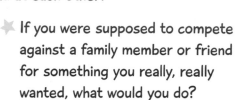

SERENA AND VENUS WILLIAMS

play a lot of tennis matches as teammates and also compete against each other.

⭐ Do you have any friends or siblings that you compete against? If so, how do you handle it? Do you ever get mad at each other?

⭐ If you were supposed to compete against a family member or friend for something you really, really wanted, what would you do?

⭐ What's more fun—playing solo or playing as one half of a pair?

VIRGINIA WOOLF

suffered greatly from depression. She found comfort in writing her thoughts down in a notebook. **How do you handle hard emotions?**

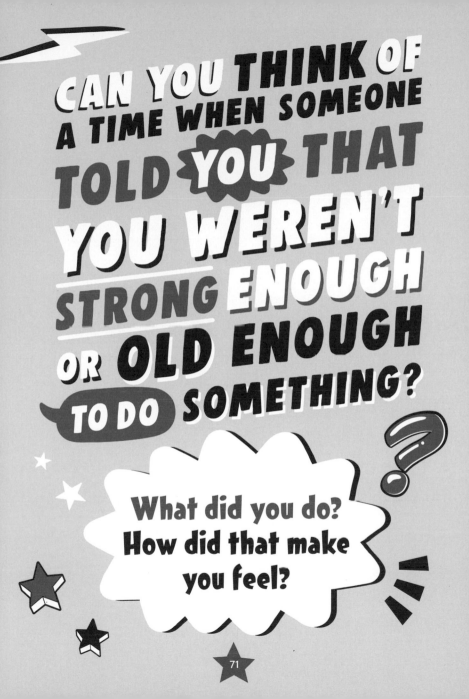

CAN YOU THINK OF A TIME WHEN SOMEONE TOLD YOU THAT YOU WEREN'T STRONG ENOUGH OR OLD ENOUGH TO DO SOMETHING?

What did you do? How did that make you feel?

MARIA REICHE was an archaeologist who loved studying the Nazca Lines, which are hundreds of lines etched into the ground in a desert in southern Peru. She wanted to know who created these mysterious ancient drawings and why.

★ Are there any artifacts, pictures, or historical mysteries that you are curious about? How can you find out more about them?

★ If you were to study artifacts, would you rather find dinosaur bones or pottery and other household objects from people who came before?

★ Would you rather explore prehistoric cave art or inspect mummies?

If you were to start a village back in time, which famous Rebel Girls would you invite to live there?

—Leni, 12, Calabasas, California, USA

SELDA BAĞCAN wrote songs about all the things she wanted to change in her homeland of Turkey. **If you were writing a protest song, what would it be about, and where would you sing it?**

POORNA MALAVATH is the youngest girl to climb Mount Everest. She was just 13 years old. It took her 52 days to get to the top!

- Have you ever set out to do something that took much longer than you'd hoped?

- What did you do to keep yourself going even when it felt hard?

- If you made it to the top of Mount Everest, what would you say or do to celebrate your achievement?

CARMEN MIRANDA

was a performer who helped make Brazilian music and dance popular around the the world. She was known for wearing bright, colorful dresses and hats with fruit on top.

⭐ Do you have a hobby or interest that you wish you could get the whole world excited about? What is it?

⭐ Do you have a signature style like Carmen?

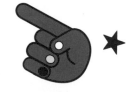

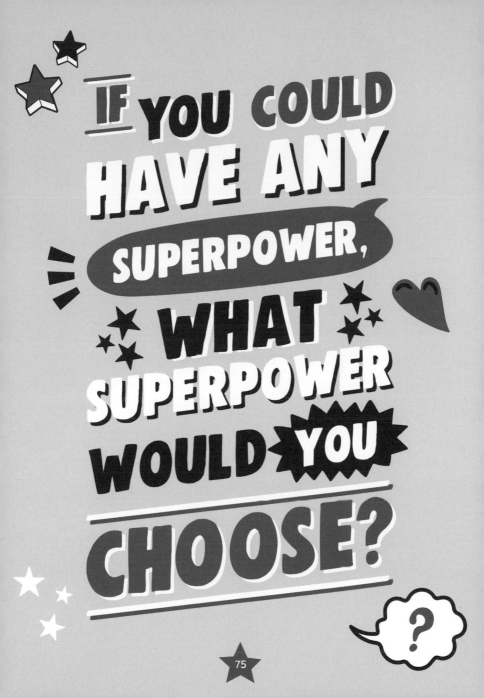

IF YOU COULD HAVE ANY SUPERPOWER, WHAT SUPERPOWER WOULD YOU CHOOSE?

MARTA VIEIRA DA SILVA is a Brazilian soccer superstar.

What is the sport for you?

BRIGID KOSGEI is a Kenyan runner who has won marathons all over the world.

CHLOE KIM is an incredible snowboarder. She was the youngest woman ever to win an Olympic gold medal in snowboarding!

Rowing or rock climbing?

Sprinting or running a marathon?

Skiing or surfing?

Soccer or softball?

Lacrosse or table tennis?

Tae kwon do or figure skating?

Gymnastics or field hockey?

Basketball or volleyball?

Bowling or fencing?

Archery or curling?

Referee a game or be a sports commentator?

ASMA KHAN

grew up in Calcutta, India. After getting married, she moved
to England, where her aunt began to teach her to cook dishes
from home. On a trip back to India, she learned even more
cooking techniques from her mom and the family cook.
Eventually Asma set aside her law degree and opened
a restaurant in London. She incorporates the familiar foods
of her childhood into the dishes she makes as a chef.

What's a food you will never get sick of eating?

What's a dish that you want to learn how to make?

What's one food that makes you think of
when you were younger?

If you opened a restaurant, what would
be your signature dish?

VIRGINIA HALL was a skilled spy who worked for the Allies during World War II. After losing her leg in a hunting accident, she wore an artificial leg that she referred to as Cuthbert. Virginia tricked her foes by wearing disguises.

★ If you were a spy, how would you disguise yourself so no one would know it was you?

★ The German secret police created a poster calling Virginia the enemy's "most dangerous spy." It showed an illustration of Virginia and said, "We must find and destroy her!" What would you do if you saw your own face on a "wanted" poster?

★ Once, Virginia escaped capture by walking for 50 miles in the mountains in the snow. It took her three days! What's the toughest or longest walk you've ever done?

> If you could bring one person back to life, who would it be?
> **—Sylvie, 12, Amsterdam, Netherlands**

ADELAIDE HERRMANN said that
"self-confidence and assurance are most essential to the successful magician."

YEAH

Do you believe in **magic?** Why or why not?

What are some things you feel **self-confident** about?

Adelaide famously convinced audiences that she could levitate, or float in the air. If you performed a magic act, would you rather convince the crowd that you could **levitate** or read people's minds?

What do you do if you have something important to say but you feel like nobody else is listening?

What's the most important part about being a good friend?

Would you rather live somewhere really hot or really cold?

?

What would you do if you found someone's wallet?

I love the story of mathematician Katherine Johnson and wish I had been there with her at NASA. Is there a famous point in time you would like to visit?

—*Ava, 9, Franklin, Massachusetts, USA*

MAGGIE TIMONEY

is an influential CEO (chief executive officer). She was a star basketball player in high school.

MEG WHITMAN

is the former CEO of Hewlett-Packard. In high school, she was the captain of her swimming team.

According to a survey, more than 90 percent of women in high-level executive positions played sports.

Why do you think playing sports might prepare someone for running a company?

Do you play sports? What have you learned from playing sports that can help you in life?

Would you rather play on a team or be the coach?

When **PEARL TRAN** and **THU GETKA** met, they realized they had a lot in common. They were both Vietnamese refugees who moved to the United States. And they both became dentists and joined the US Navy before meeting each other!

- Have you ever had a neat coincidence with a friend?

- Do you believe certain people are destined to meet each other?

- Would you rather be a dentist or a deep-sea fisherman?

Would you rather go back in time or to the future?
—*Celia, 9, Wilmington, Delaware, USA*

MANAL AL-SHARIF

started a women's rights movement in Saudi Arabia
when she made a video of herself driving a car, even though
women were forbidden to drive in her home country.

Do women still need to fight for their
rights in your country or region?

Has anyone ever tried to make you feel
"less than" because of your gender?

What would you say to someone who thought that
women should not have the same rights as men?

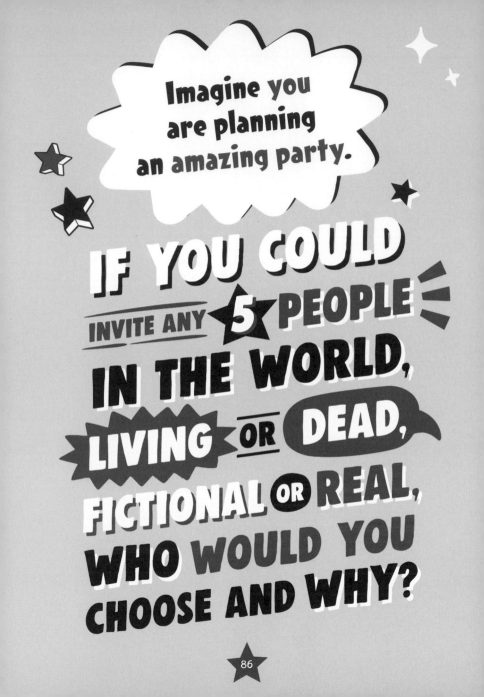

Imagine you are planning an amazing party.

IF YOU COULD INVITE ANY 5 PEOPLE IN THE WORLD, LIVING OR DEAD, FICTIONAL OR REAL, WHO WOULD YOU CHOOSE AND WHY?

YOUNG JEAN LEE writes exciting experimental plays. She is the first Asian American woman to have a play produced on Broadway.

Would you rather write plays or act in them? Be seen onstage or do work behind the scenes?

Would you rather have the major role in a local production or a small part in a Broadway show?

If you could write a play about any event in history, what would you pick?

What is the best play you've ever seen or read? Why did you like it so much?

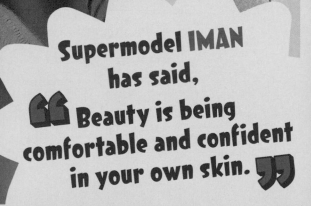

What makes you feel beautiful?

Where are you and what are you doing when you feel the most confident?

Famous runway models become well-known for their distinct runway walks. If you were a model, what would your unique walk look like?

Would you rather be a fashion model or a fashion designer?

If you were in a fashion show, what types of clothing would you like to model?

PEGGY GUGGENHEIM inherited a big fortune, and with it she curated a world-famous collection of modern art.

- If you inherited or won a lot of money, what would you spend it on?

- If you could make a collection of anything, from cookies to race cars, what would it be and why?

GERDA TARO was a photographer who documented the Spanish Civil War and its effects on the people who lived through it.

- What's something happening today that you'd want to photograph so people could learn about it?

- Do you learn better by reading or looking at photographs?

If you could get a tattoo, what would it be and why?

If you found out you had four hours to put together a dinner party for eight people, what would you do?

If you had to choose between going to school for five days a week all year long or going to school for seven days a week but getting the summers off, which would you choose? Weekends off or summers off?

Would you rather write songs or sing them?

—Ellie, 8, Medford, Massachusetts, USA

SAMANTHA POWER witnessed a terrible war in Bosnia as a young journalist. Afterward, she wrote a book that won a Pulitzer Prize.

LEYMAH GBOWEE won a Nobel Peace Prize for her work helping to end the Liberian Civil War.

YUAN YUAN TAN is a talented ballerina. She's won many awards, including an Isadora Duncan Dance Award for Outstanding Achievement in Performance.

What other prizes would you create? Who would you give them to?

Who would you give each of these awards to?

Best Knock-Knock Jokester

Most Likely to Own a Pet Snake

Crabbiest Morning Person

Best Song Lip-Syncher

Most Entertaining Babysitter

Luckiest Board Game Player

Best Pancake Maker

Most Forgetful

Loudest Snorer

Most Convincing Cat Impression

RUTH BADER GINSBURG was a US Supreme

Court Justice for 27 years. She listened to lawyers' arguments and helped make important legal decisions about pollution, voting rights, same-sex marriage, civil rights, gender discrimination, the rights of people with disabilities, and many other topics.

⭐ Picture yourself in a courtroom. Would you rather be a lawyer or a judge?

⭐ How would you feel about making decisions that could affect so many people's lives?

⭐ Before joining the Supreme Court, Ruth was the first woman to be hired as a tenured professor at Columbia Law School. Getting tenure is like being guaranteed a job for life. If you were to teach one subject for your whole life, what subject would you choose?

LOWRI MORGAN is an ultramarathon runner who has run through jungles and the Arctic. She has faced bears, jaguars, and snakes and even swum through water filled with piranhas.

- Does this sound exciting or terrifying to you?

- What is the hardest physical challenge you've ever had to push through?

- Thoughts on piranhas? "Eh, I'm not worried. Those fish with razor-sharp teeth don't really bite humans" or "Er, no thanks, I'd rather run a zillion miles around that lake?"

If you could ask your favorite Rebel Girl a question, what would you ask?

—*Leonora, 7, Chevy Chase, Maryland, USA*

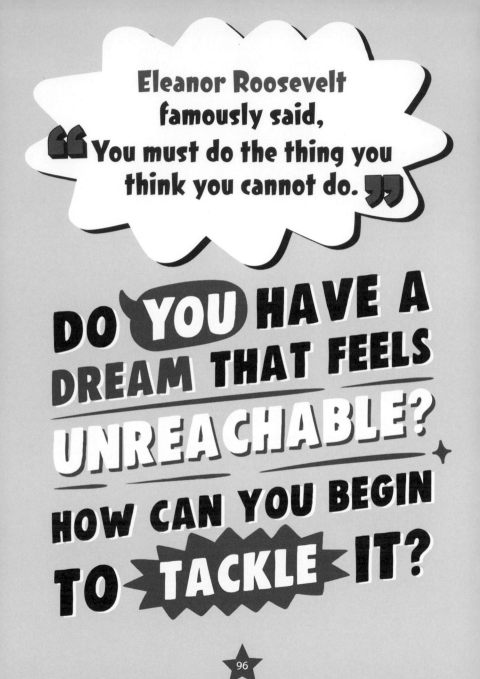

Eleanor Roosevelt famously said, "You must do the thing you think you cannot do."

DO YOU HAVE A DREAM THAT FEELS UNREACHABLE? HOW CAN YOU BEGIN TO TACKLE IT?

FLORENCE CHADWICK was such a strong swimmer that she could have gone to the Olympics, but she thought pools were boring. She only liked swimming in the open sea, where the waves and the fish and the unpredictability of the ocean were exciting!

- Where do you like swimming more—in a pool or in an ocean or lake? (And if you don't like swimming at all, why is that?)

- Would you rather swim a mile or do cartwheels for a mile?

- At the beach, would you rather build a sandcastle or swim in the water? Learn how to sail or learn how to surf?

Would you give up cars to save the environment?
—*Steliana Rose, 11, Concord, California, USA*

AMEENAH GURIB-FAKIM is a biodiversity scientist, dedicated to learning all about the amazing plants found on Mauritius, the tiny island nation she calls home. She works to find out which ones might be used as food, medicine, and more. In 2015, she became the first female president of her country!

★ If you could grow a giant field of any plant, what would you choose?

★ If you could be any flower, tree, or other plant, what would you be and why?

ARIANNA HUFFINGTON worked so hard as the CEO (chief executive officer) of a company that she suffered from extreme exhaustion called "burnout."

★ Have you ever worked so hard at something that you felt exhausted?

★ What is something you like to do in the middle of your day to feel rested and refreshed?

REYNA DUONG

owns a shop where she serves Vietnamese sandwiches,
or "banh mi." A traditional banh mi is often pork (or other meat)
with pickled carrots and radishes, sliced cucumbers, cilantro, and
mayonnaise on a baguette. It might be spicy or not.

What are your three favorite sandwich ingredients?

What's something you never, ever want in a sandwich?

What's the most unusual sandwich you've ever heard of?

What's the coolest sandwich you've ever tried?

Do these questions make you want to eat a sandwich?

MADAME SAQUI was a celebrated tightrope walker in France, beloved for her courage and grace.

ANNA OLGA ALBERTINA BROWN was a famous aerialist who swung and spun high in the air—often hanging by her teeth!

If you ran away with an old-time circus, what would be your act?

Tightrope walker or bodybuilder?

Ringmaster or mime?

Ride a unicycle or drive the clown car?

Juggle fire or walk on stilts?

Acrobat or trapeze artist?

Twist into impossible shapes as a contortionist
or speak through a dummy as a ventriloquist?

Escape artist or human cannonball?

Make balloon animals or walk on your hands?

Knife thrower or knife
thrower's volunteer?

Some TV characters have a catchphrase they say whenever they come into a room or when they do something silly. If you were a TV character, what would your catchphrase be?

Would you rather write a paper about ancient Egypt or the Wild West? Why?

Would it be harder for you to give up soda or cheese? (Don't forget about pizza!)

Would it be harder for you to give up watching YouTube or give up eating meat?

GLORIA STEINEM is a famous feminist. What does the word *feminist* mean to you? **Do you consider yourself a feminist? Why or why not?**

STACEY ABRAMS is a writer, politician, and activist. In just two years, she helped register 800,000 voters in her home state of Georgia.

⭐ Do you think voting is important? At what age do you think people should be able to vote?

⭐ Stacey has written nonfiction books and a legal thriller under her own name. She has also written romance novels under a pen name. If you wrote in any genre of fiction, which would you choose? Romance or sci-fi? Mystery or fantasy? Fairy tale or horror? Historical fiction or humor?

⭐ If you wrote under a fake name, what name would you pick?

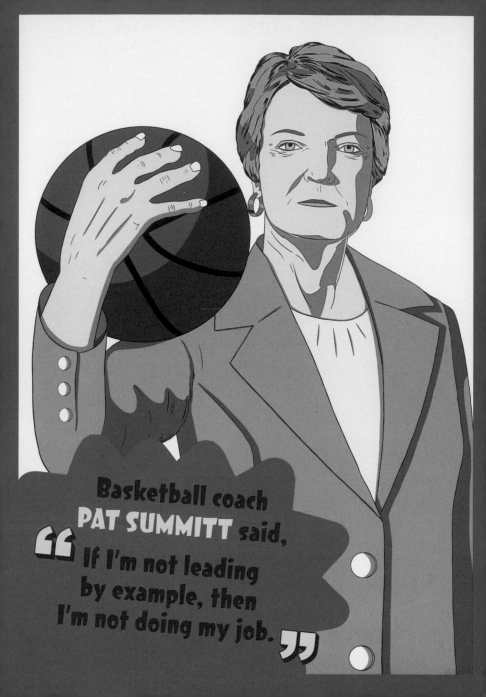

Do you have younger siblings or know any younger kids? What is something you hope younger people pick up from you?

Who do you look up to? Why?

If you could pick anyone in the world to be your mentor, who would you pick?

Pat was beloved for supporting and uplifting her players. She was also known for yelling and screaming and pushing her athletes hard. Do you think it is more effective to yell at people or say positive things to encourage them?

If you had the power to delete three letters from the alphabet, which ones would you choose? How would you pronounce words that used to have those letters? How would you make yourself understood?

Do you find it hard to keep secrets?

What's the craziest dream you've ever had?

When was the last time you lol'd?

Do you believe in yourself? You should!

—*Claire, 11, Platte City, Missouri, USA*

Pauline Léon was a revolutionary in France who started a group called *femmes sans culottes*, which means "women without breeches."

IF **YOU** STARTED A REVOLUTIONARY GROUP, WHAT WOULD **YOU** CALL **IT?**

What's your favorite dessert and what is one modification you would make to it to make it unique? What's your favorite dinner food and what is one modification you would make to it to make it unique?

—*Eloisa, 7, Madison, Wisconsin, USA*

ELEANOR ROOSEVELT was a driving force

behind the creation of a document called the Universal Declaration of Human Rights.

⭐ What rights do you think all humans should have?

⭐ As a teenager, Eleanor went to school in England, where a teacher named Marie Souvestre boosted her confidence, encouraged her independence, and inspired her to think about social justice. Have you ever had a teacher like Marie who changed your life? What did this teacher do to inspire you?

108

Artist **FRIDA KAHLO** was in a terrible accident when she was 18 years old. She spent months in bed healing. Using a special easel, she learned to paint while lying down. She created many colorful self-portraits. In these paintings, she is often wearing flowers in her hair and surrounded by monkeys, parrots, dogs, or some of the other animals she kept as pets.

If you were laid up in bed for months, what would you do to pass the time?

If you painted a self-portrait, what other things would you include in the picture? What would those things tell people about you?

Frida spent most of her life in her childhood home, which was known as the Blue House for its brightly colored exterior. If you could paint where you live any color or pattern, what would you choose?

XIYE BASTIDA fights for climate justice. She helps organize youth climate strikes.

KRISTAL AMBROSE is also an environmental activist. She convinced the Bahamian government to ban single-use plastics to reduce plastic pollution around the island.

There are so many ways to help the planet. How would you like to help the environment?

110

Organize a school strike for climate awareness or plan a beach cleanup?

Bike everywhere or take only public transportation?

Become a vegetarian or never use take-out containers?

Grow all your own veggies or raise your own chickens for food?

Use no electricity one day a week or buy no new outfits for a year?

Give up using plastic bottles or give up buying books and read only library books?

Host a bake sale and donate money to an environmental organization or set up a compost bin?

Buy only used clothing or make your own soap and shampoo?

Reduce air-conditioning use in the summer or lower the heat in the winter?

Give up TV four nights a week or conserve water by restricting showers to just three minutes?

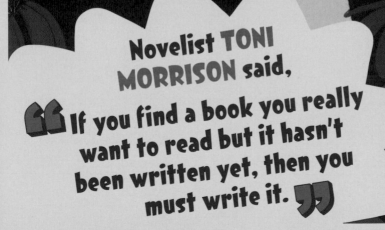

Novelist **TONI MORRISON** said,

"If you find a book you really want to read but it hasn't been written yet, then you must write it."

What is your favorite book? Why is it so special to you?

If you could be a character in any book you've ever read, what character would you pick?

If you could choose a character from a book to join your family, who would you choose?

Imagine you are writing a book. What would the story be about? Would you put a character just like you in your story?

SUSAN POLGAR'S

father trained her and her sisters to become chess champions. He believed any child could become a "genius" in whatever they put their mind to. **Do you think people are born geniuses, or do they need to cultivate their talent to become a genius?**

JULIA LÓPEZ

worked on her parents' farm as a child, before taking off for Mexico City, where she taught herself how to paint. Eventually, she became a celebrated artist who exhibited her art all around the world. She often painted vibrant pictures of girls in long dresses, horses in flowery fields, and other scenes from her childhood in rural Mexico.

⭐ What's something you've created that you'd want exhibited in a museum?

⭐ If you drew or painted pictures to show off your hometown, what would you put in them?

Marie Tharp was a geologist who studied the ocean floor to figure out how the continents were drifting apart.

IF YOU COULD STUDY ONE PART OF THE EARTH, WHAT WOULD IT BE? WHY?

KERRI STRUG was an incredible gymnast. During the 1996 Olympics, she landed awkwardly after a vault and hurt her ankle. But she had one more vault to do. And if she did it well, her whole team would win a gold medal! She had to decide if she'd compete in her final vault or sit it out. She went for it! She ran toward the vault, flew into the air, spinning and twisting, and managed to land without falling. Proud, but in pain, she was carried off the mat while fans cheered madly. Kerri helped her team secure the gold but was unable to compete in any other events because of her injury.

⭐ Knowing that you might hurt yourself further, would you do the same thing?

⭐ What would you consider while making that decision?

⭐ Do you think being surrounded by a huge audience would affect your choice?

⭐ What would you say to Kerri if you ever had the chance to meet her?

GRACE O'MALLEY wanted to be a pirate, but her father said that was just for boys. So, Grace cut off all her hair and became "Bald Grace" to prove she was just as fierce and ready for action.

* Would you ever want to be a pirate? Why or why not?

* What does your hair mean to you? Would it be a big deal to cut it all off?

* If you could have any hair style, what would it be?

When **VIOLA DAVIS** was starting out as a stage actor, she had terrible stage fright. Sometimes, she would just clam up, and no one could make her say a single word. She pushed through it and became one of the most celebrated actors in the world.

* Have you ever experienced stage fright? What did you do?

* If you could play any part in a TV show or movie, what would it be?

* Who would you want to play you in the movie of your life?

Do you wish you could live somewhere different from where you live now? Where?

—Hazel, 5, Union City, Pennsylvania, USA

What are some lessons you've learned outside of school?

If you had to wear one item every time you left the house for a year, which would you pick—clown shoes on your feet or wool mittens on your hands?

Does your family have any holiday traditions? If you could create a new tradition, what would it be?

Would you rather trim shrubs into cool animal shapes or make ice sculptures?

Malala Yousafzai has said, " Education is power for women. "

HOW DO YOU USE YOUR EDUCATION TO FEEL POWERFUL?

MARY BARRA is the CEO of General Motors. She has said, "If you have a problem, you've got to solve it. Because that problem is going to get bigger."

Are you good at solving problems? What's a problem that you are proud you solved?

What's a problem that you wish you had solved better or more quickly?

If you could snap your fingers and solve one problem in your life or in the world, no matter how big or small, what would it be?

Mary has worked in the auto industry her whole life. She knows everything about cars. If you could learn everything in the world about one business, what would you pick?

Would you rather be shrunk down to the size of a mouse or grow to be 20 feet tall? Would your answer be different if you were to change sizes for only one day?

You can use only one condiment on your food for the rest of your life. What do you pick?

Do you keep a diary? Why or why not?

What's your favorite daydream?

If you were Ruby Bridges, how would it feel to have people protecting you and other people trying to scare you?

—Aemelia, 7, Springfield, Pennsylvania, USA

SAMANTHA CRISTOFORETTI is

the first astronaut to brew espresso in space.

⭐ Picture your name in the history books. You are the first person to do something. What is it?

⭐ If you went to space, what's the one thing you'd HAVE to take with you?

VIVIAN MAIER was a fantastic photographer who

managed to capture people's feelings in her photos.

⭐ If you were taking a picture of how you feel right now, what would you put in the picture?

⭐ If you could travel anywhere in the world to take photos, where would you go?

⭐ Would you rather take pictures of people or landscapes? Wildlife or fashion? Celebrities or breaking news? Protests or vacation getaways?

For **BESSIE COLEMAN**, life was all about planes! She was the first Black American woman and first Native American to earn a pilot's license.

JESSICA WATSON sailed around the world on her own when she was just 16 years old! The sailboat was her vehicle of choice.

BESSIE STRINGFIELD crisscrossed the country on her motorcycle at a time when the United States was still segregated and it was considered very "unladylike" to ride a motorcycle. She visited all 48 states on the continent, often sleeping under the stars.

How would you like to get around?

Ride a motorcycle or ride a horse?

Pilot a helicopter or go parasailing?

Drive a fire engine or drive an ambulance?

Compete in a three-legged race or
race on a tandem bicycle?

Drive a pickup truck or cruise
around in a convertible?

Row a rowboat or crew a sailboat?

Drive a taxi or drive a bus?

Parachute out of a plane or operate a forklift?

Skateboard everywhere or hop on a ski lift?

Take a tram through the sky or
ride on a hot-air balloon?

HORTENSIA was a brilliant speaker in ancient Rome who could persuade people to change their minds. She convinced countless people to speak up for themselves.

- Have you ever felt like you needed to speak up for yourself more? Why did you or didn't you?

- If you could go back in time to a particular moment, what would you say to defend yourself?

- Who do you know who is really persuasive and good at changing people's minds?

AUDREY HEPBURN

was an actress who was born in Brussels and raised in Belgium, England, and the Netherlands. Sometimes when she played a character, she had to speak with an accent.

Have you ever tried to speak with an accent?
How did you learn it?

If you were cast in a movie and had to speak
in an accent, what would you do?

Audrey also performed on stage. There's an old
superstition in the theater where actors believe it is bad
luck to say "good luck." Instead they say "break a leg."
Can you think of any other superstitions?
Do you believe in them? Why or why not?

Would you rather have unlimited access to money but always be grumpy or always be cheerful but have little money?

★

Imagine you are a Greek god or goddess. Which one would you be? Why?

★

If you could shape-shift into any animal, what would you choose?

★

Would you rather create a board game or a video game?

YEAH

What mistake have you made that you regret the most? How did you keep going?
—*Myka, 9, Oberlin, Ohio, USA*

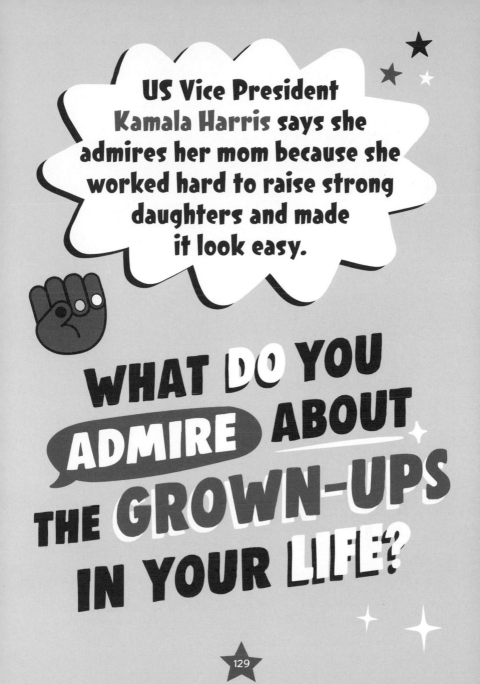

US Vice President Kamala Harris says she admires her mom because she worked hard to raise strong daughters and made it look easy.

WHAT DO YOU ADMIRE ABOUT THE GROWN-UPS IN YOUR LIFE?

EMILIE SNETHLAGE
explored remote sections of
the Amazon rain forest.

MARY KINGSLEY
was the first woman to climb
Mount Cameroon.

What kind of an adventurer are you?

Climb a mountain or explore a desert?

Trek through a rain forest or cross a savanna?

Ski to the South Pole or sail down the Nile?

Go solo or travel in a pack?

Ride a camel or drive a dogsled?

Scale a rock face or gallop on a horse?

Use a compass or follow the stars?

Carry a heavy pack or hunt and
gather your own food?

Build a tent or build a fire?

Parachute from a helicopter
or walk the whole way?

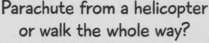

CELIA CRUZ was the Queen of Salsa.
BEYONCÉ is a pop superstar.
And **ROXANNE SHANTÉ** is an amazing rapper.

If you could be a singing sensation,
what type of music would you sing?

If you could perform a duet with
anyone in the world, who would it be?

If your family formed a band together, who would be
the lead singer? Who would play which instruments?

If you showed up to play a concert and
all the power went out, what would you do?

Do you prefer to be the leader of a group or a member of the group?

★

Would you rather wear a top hat every day for a year or a tool belt every day for a year?

★

Would you rather decorate 1,000 cupcakes or make 1,000 beaded necklaces?

★

If you could watch only animated shows or only live-action shows for an entire year, which would you choose?

Would you want to be a pirate leader, Egyptian queen, or a Greek goddess?

—Vivian, 11, Dallas, Texas, USA

In an interview, poet AMANDA GORMAN said, " Poetry has never been the language of barriers, it's always been the language of bridges. "

Do you believe that poetry can help bring people together?

Can you think of a poem that has challenged you or made you feel? What is it?

If you were selected to write and deliver a poem at the presidential inauguration, what would you write about? How would you prepare for your big moment?

Do you like silence? Why or why not?

★

Which title would you rather have: food-fight champion of the universe or world's best ventriloquist?

★

Would you rather be a hilarious joke teller or an unbeatable card player?

★

What would be tougher for you: not speaking a word for a month or not using any electronics for a month?

★

What dish would you create to win a TV food competition?

Sonia Sotomayor had the nickname "Ají" or "hot pepper" when she was little. What is your nickname?

—Hannah, 6, Washington, DC, USA

When **SANDRA AGUEBOR-EKPERUOH** announced that she wanted to be a mechanic, her parents thought, *No way! A garage is no place for a girl!*

What would you do if you and your parents disagreed about what you should study or what path you should pursue? What would you say to them?

What are some careers that interest you? What are some accomplishments you would like to achieve?

When you think about the future, what is most important to you?

What's your science style?

BRENDA MILNER

is a neuropsychologist. She studies the brain and how people behave.

KATIA KRAFFT

was a volcanologist. She studied volcanoes.

Research people's brains or
Earth's volcanoes?

Study volcanoes on Earth or
volcanoes on Venus?

Work in a lab or in the field?

Be an archaeologist or an astronomer?

Study whales or eagles? Toads or sloths?
Hyenas or bears?

Master computer science or
climate science?

Create robots or vaccines?

Become a botanist and study plants or
a malacologist and study snails?

Build a bridge or a microchip?

Study how flies see or how bats hear?

Become a meteorologist and track the weather
or a seismologist and track earthquakes?

OPRAH WINFREY said, "You get in life what you have the courage to ask for."

What's the **hardest** thing you've ever asked for?

What's something you want but are scared of asking for?

What is the most courageous thing you've ever done?

?

Illustration Credits

Acacia Rodriguez - USA, 114B

Aisha Akeju - USA, 39

Alexandra Bowman - USA, 8

Alice Barberini - Italy, 35

Alice Beniero - Italy, 130R

Alice Piaggio - Switzerland, 68

Alleanna Harris - USA, 55, 64T

Amalteia - Portugal, 57B

Ana Juan - Spain, 70B

Annalisa Ventura - Italy, 9, 76TL, 83L, 83R, 103T, 116, 126

Ashleigh Corrin - USA, 51

Barbara Dziadosz - Germany, 19T

Beatrice Cerocchi - Italy, 28T

Bodil Jane - Netherlands, 130L

Camille de Cussac - France, 80

Cindy Echevarria - USA, 56

Claire Idera - Nigeria, 88

Cristina Amodeo - Italy, 28B

Cristina Portolano - Italy, 18, 31B, 64B

Dalila Rovazzani - Italy, 79

Danielle Elysse Mann - USA, 62

Data Oruwari - Nigeria, 76RM

Debora Guidi - Italy, 70T

Eleanor Davis - USA, 94

Elena de Santi - Spain, 48

Elenia Beretta - Italy, 114T

Eline Van Dam - Netherlands 52, 132M

Elisabetta Stoinich - Italy, 6

Elizabeth Baddeley - USA, 29

Eva Rust - Switzerland, 40M

Fanesha Fabre - USA, 120, 132R

Fanny Blanc - France, 98B

Gaia Stella - Italy, 72

Geraldine Sy - Philippines, 40B, 98T

Giulia Flamini - Italy, 22, 40T

Giulia Tomai - Italy, 24B, 73T, 123T

Helena Morais Soares - Portugal, 109

Jacquelyn B. Moore - USA, 104

Jeanne Detallante - Belgium, 16

Jennifer Potter - USA, 60B

Jenny Meilihove - Israel, 11

Joana Estrela - Portugal, 20B

Johnalynn Holland - USA, 49R, 117B

Jonell Joshua - USA, 137

Justine Lecouffe - USA, 57T

Kate Prior - USA, 85, 90T

Kathrin Honesta - Indonesia, 117T, 124TR

Kelsee Thomas - USA, 103B

Keturah Ariel - USA, 110R, 134

Kim Holt - USA, 124B

Laura Junger - France, 100T

Lea Heinrich - Germany, 47R

Liekeland - Netherlands, 36

Lisa Lanoë - France, 67B

Lizzy Stewart - UK, 108

Maïté Franchi - France, 42

Marina Muun - Austria, 50B

Marta Giunipero - Italy, 90B

Marta Signori - Italy, 47L, 50T, 60T, 127

Martina Paukova - Slovakia, 49L, 138B

Marylou Faure - UK, 65, 138T

Michelle D'Urbano - Zambia, 24T

Monica Ahanonu - USA, 12, 31T

Nan Lawson - USA, 67T

Naomi Anderson-Subryan - UK, 20M

Noa Denmon - USA, 25, 112

Noa Snir - Israel, 97

Paola Rollo - Italy, 78

Petra Braun - Austria, 92BL

Ping Zhu - USA, 132L

Priya Kuriyan - India, 73

Queenbe Monyei - USA, 17

Salini Perera - Canada, 76B, 87

Sally Caulwell - Ireland, 20T

Sally Deng - USA, 110L

Sally Nixon - USA, 37

Sara Olmos - Spain, 123B

Sarah Loulendo - France, 92TL

Sarah Madden - UK, 4, 59

Sarah Wilkins - New Zealand, 32, 95

Sonia Lazo - El Salvador, 74

Sophia Martineck - Germany, 45

Stephanie Singleton - Canada, 99

T. S. Abe - UK, 140

Thandiwe Tshabalala - South Africa, 92R

Toni D. Chambers - USA, 100L, 124TL

Valencia Spates - USA, 84

Zozia Dzierżawska - Poland, 19B

In the credits above, T=top, B=bottom, L=left, R=right, M=middle

About Rebel Girls

Rebel Girls is a global, multi-platform empowerment brand dedicated to inspiring and instilling confidence in a generation of girls around the world through content, experiences, products, and community. Orginating from an international best-selling children's book, Rebel Girls amplifies stories of real-life, extraordinary women throughout history, geography, and field of excellence. With a growing community of 16 million self-identified Rebel Girls spanning more than 100 countries, the brand engages with the Alpha Generation through its book series, award-winning podcast, app, events, and merchandise.

Join the Rebel Girls' community:
Facebook: facebook.com/rebelgirls
Instagram: @rebelgirls
Twitter: @rebelgirlsbook
Web: rebelgirls.com
Podcast: rebelgirls.com/podcast

If you liked this book, please take a moment to review it wherever you prefer!

ENJOY OTHER REBEL GIRLS BOOKS!

Read about amazing women from all over the world and throughout history.

Let their stories inspire you to dream big, aim high, and stay Rebel!